05/2005 $18.95   972.9
                                                 Car

20th Century
PERSPECTIVES

The Cuban Missile Crisis

E.J. Carter

Heinemann Library
Chicago, Illinois

© 2004 Reed Educational & Professional Publishing
Published by Heinemann Library,
an imprint of Reed Educational & Professional Publishing,
Chicago, Illinois

Customer Service 888-454-2279

Visit our website at www.heinemannlibrary.com

Designed by Herman Adler Design
Printed in the United States by Lake Book Manufacturing, Inc.

08 07 06 05 04
10 9 8 7 6 5 4 3 2 1

Library of Congress Cataloging-in-Publication Data
Carter, E. J., 1971–
   The Cuban Missile Crisis / E.J. Carter.
      v. cm. -- (20th century perspectives)
Includes bibliographical references and index.
Contents: What was the Cuban Missile Crisis? -- From Revolution to Totalitarianism -- The Cold War -- Castro and the Cuban Revolution -- JFK and the Election of 1960 -- Disaster at the Bay of Pigs -- Sparring in Vienna and Berlin -- Arming Cuba -- Ex-Comm -- Invasion vs. blockade -- Going public -- Diplomacy -- Eyeball to eyeball -- The Jupiters -- A possible solution -- New tensions -- The secret missile swap -- Doomsday scenarios -- Changing historical evaluations -- 1989 -- Timeline.
   ISBN 1-4034-3806-4 (library binding-hardcover) -- ISBN 1-4034-4180-4 (pbk.)
   1. Cuban Missile Crisis, 1962--Juvenile literature. [1. Cuban Missile Crisis, 1962.] I. Title. II. Series.
   E841.C325 2003
   972.9106'4--dc21
                                        2003009552

Acknowledgments
The author and publishers are grateful to the following for permission to reproduce copyright material:
p. 4 AMR; pp. 5, 13, 16, 17, 36 AP/Wide World; pp. 6, 41 Hulton Deutsch Collection/Corbis; pp. 7, 8, 15, 20, 24, 32, 37, 39 Hulton Archive by Getty Images; pp. 9, 10, 11, 12, 14, 19, 21, 25, 26, 27, 28, 29, 30, 40; pp. 18, 22, 23, 33, 35, 38 Corbis; p. 31 U.S. Army; p. 34 Aero Graphics, Inc/Corbis; p. 42 Peter Turnley/Corbis; p. 43 Robert Maass/Corbis

Cover photo reproduced with permission of Corbis

Contents

What Was the Cuban Missile Crisis?

This map of Europe after World War II shows the line dividing the continent, called the Iron Curtain. Arrows show Red Army (USSR) advances in Eastern Europe which established USSR control.

The Cuban Missile Crisis was the most dangerous moment of the Cold War, and the closest the world has ever come to nuclear war. On October 15, 1962, the United States learned that the Soviet Union (USSR) had placed nuclear warheads on Cuban soil, only 90 miles (145 kilometers) from Florida. These weapons could possibly strike any spot in the continental United States, a thought which terrified the U.S. government and many Americans. Over the next thirteen days, the U.S. insisted that the missiles be removed. The world held its breath while it waited for the conflict to be resolved.

The Cuban Missile Crisis can be seen as a turning point in the Cold War—the first time people recognized just how dangerous the world had become. The Cold War lasted more than 40 years, from the end of World War II to the fall of the USSR in 1991. It was a struggle between two very different ideas of how political and economic policies should be made. Capitalist countries like the United States and its allies in Western Europe were committed to the free market. Goods would be exchanged for money in the market with very little government interference. The countries also favored democratic forms of government that defended free speech, freedom of religion, and freedom to protest against the state. In communist nations like the USSR, the state controlled most economic activity, and the Communist Party made political decisions for the working-class or "proletariat." Communism tried to make all its citizens economically equal, although high-ranking officials in the party often enjoyed special privileges that citizens could not.

Key

— The Iron Curtain
→ Advance of the Red Army 1944–45
Communist countries
Communist but not under control of USSR
Capitalist democratic countries

NB: Austria was occupied by the U.S., USSR, Britain, and France until 1955 when it became independent.

N W E S

NORWAY

SWEDEN

North Sea

DENMARK

Baltic Sea

Moscow•

BRITAIN

Stettin•

Berlin•

NETH.

EAST GERMANY

POLAND

UNION OF SOVIET SOCIALIST REPUBLICS (USSR)

BELGIUM

LUX.

WEST GERMANY

CZECHOSLOVAKIA

FRANCE

SWITZERLAND

AUSTRIA

HUNGARY

•Trieste

ROMANIA

YUGOSLAVIA

Black Sea

ITALY

BULGARIA

ALBANIA

GREECE

TURKEY

0 — 250 km
0 — 125 miles

Mediterranean Sea

Throughout the Cold War, the two sides struggled without actually fighting. Each side tried to convince other nations to adopt their form of government, but they avoided military confrontation. In 1962, however, only diplomacy, courage, and compromise prevented war from breaking out. The U.S. president, John F. Kennedy, was a young leader without much experience in foreign affairs. The Soviet leader, Nikita Khrushchev, was committed both to reforming the USSR and to challenging U.S. power. Together Khrushchev and Kennedy were faced with the difficult task of avoiding disaster by controlling calls within their own countries to launch a war. Over the two weeks of the crisis, and in the months afterward, Kennedy and Khrushchev exchanged 22 letters and numerous secret messages through their aides. They each made concessions to the other's position while defending their nations' interests.

The Cuban Missile Crisis is an event that reveals how presidents and their advisors make decisions under pressure. It tells us a great deal about the inner workings of our political system, as well as that of the now-gone USSR. The crisis was also perhaps John F. Kennedy's greatest achievement. After his assassination in 1963, he was transformed into a hero in the eyes of many Americans. The Cuban Missile Crisis lets us examine Kennedy's achievements, as well as his faults and failings. For all of these reasons, the Crisis has become one of the most frequently studied topics in American history.

East German soldiers building the Berlin Wall in 1961 to stop East Germans from escaping to the West. The wall increased Cold War tension that nearly turned to disaster in the Cuban Missile Crisis.

Nikita Khrushchev, the USSR leader

Nikita Khrushchev was born in 1894 in a small village between Russia and the Ukraine. As a boy he was a shepherd, then at sixteen he began working as a coal miner. After the Russian Revolution in 1917, Khrushchev was able to go to school for a while, and later became active in politics. In 1949, he was named secretary of the Central Committee, which made him one of the most powerful people in the USSR. In 1953, a struggle broke out to decide who would be the new ruler. By 1956 Khrushchev was in charge.

From Revolution to Totalitarianism

Communism is an economic and political theory which argues that workers should control the government. One important communist thinker was Karl Marx, a German writer who lived in the mid-19th century. Marx believed that all of history was a struggle between the upper and lower classes, and that eventually the working-class—the "proletariat"—would lead a revolution to claim power.

The first communist government appeared in Russia in 1917. The Bolshevik Party, under Vladimir Lenin and Leon Trotsky, took control of the country and created a "dictatorship of the proletariat." Soon after a brutal civil war, Lenin died, and a power struggle for leadership of the Communist Party broke out. In 1927, Josef Stalin gained control of the government and exiled Trotsky and his followers.

Vladimir Lenin, the main leader of the Bolshevik Party and ruler of the USSR from the Russian Revolution in 1917 until his death in 1924.

Totalitarianism

Under Stalin the Soviet Union—the new regime's full name was Union of Soviet Socialist Republics, or USSR—began an ambitious program to industrialize the largely agricultural nation as rapidly as possible. Stalin outlined a series of Five Year Plans that set goals for economic growth that required tremendous hardship and sacrifice among the Soviet people. To help meet these goals, Stalin expanded the series of labor camps established during the civil war into a terrifying system known as the Gulag Archipelago.

Monstrous prison camps

Rumors of the horrors of Stalin's regime occasionally appeared during the 1930s, 40s, and 50s in reports by people who escaped it. But the study that brought the world's attention was a book by Alexandr Solzenitsyn called *The Gulag Archipelago*, published in the 1960s. It was based on his own experiences in the prisons and labor camps, as well as numerous discussions with other survivors. In three very thick volumes, Solzenitsyn described the entire system, from the moment the police knocked on a person's door to being questioned at the police station, which often involved torture. He went on to discuss the different labor camps and the millions of people who died in them, as well as prisoners who resisted the system and tried to destroy it.

Hundreds of prison labor camps were set up all over the country to build roads, bridges, and railroads, cut timber, and dig up minerals from the earth. Some of the prisoners in these camps were ordinary criminals and petty thieves, but most of them were people who criticized the government or were suspected of hostility to the working class. Conditions in the Gulag were extremely bad and millions of people died from starvation, cold, overwork, and disease. Millions more died in a program to transform small, privately-owned farms into large enterprises managed by bureaucracies, a process known as collectivization.

To strengthen his power and prevent opposition, Stalin also carried out the Great Purges during the 1930s. Members of the Bolshevik Party who were seen as a threat to Stalin were removed from power, put on trial, and executed. They were replaced with younger people who Stalin could control and rely on. Gradually, Stalin built a totalitarian state in which private property was banned, free speech was censored, and all challenges to Stalin were crushed.

This is a poster from the Soviet Union during the Cold War. It says, "The Five Year Plan in Four Years." It urged Soviet citizens to work hard enough to produce in four years what would normally take five years to produce.

World War II

Despite the brutality of the Soviet regime, Nazi Germany was a greater threat to Europe and the U.S. during the 1930s. After Adolph Hitler came to power in 1933, the Germans rapidly built up their military in preparation for a war of conquest. In 1938, Hitler took over Austria and threatened to absorb a large piece of Czechoslovakia. Instead of responding to this aggression, British and French leaders adopted a policy of "appeasement." At the Munich Conference in September they gave in to Hitler's demands in order to avoid going to war. But appeasing Hitler did not work. In March 1939, the Germans took the rest of Czechoslovakia, and in September they invaded Poland, launching World War II. Memory of the failed policy of appeasement played a big role in the Cuban Missile Crisis. U.S. leaders did not want to be compared to those British and French leaders.

History's lesson

The Munich Agreement gave to Nazi Germany the part of Czechoslovakia known as the Sudentenland, where many German-speaking people lived. The Agreement called for the Czechs to abandon the territory by October 10—only eleven days after the agreement was signed. In some territories, the people would be allowed to vote on whether they wanted to join Germany. The Munich Agreement even called for the Czechs to "release Sudenten German prisoners who are serving terms of imprisonment for political offenses." The document was signed by Adolf Hitler, Neville Chamberlain (Britain), Eduard Daladier (France), and Benito Mussolini (Italy).

The Cold War

During World War II, the United States and its allies fought together with the Soviet Union (USSR) against the Germans. In fact, many of the toughest battles of the war were fought and won by the Soviets, and they suffered far greater losses than the western powers. Around 20 million Soviet troops and citizens died during the war. After Germany had been defeated, it was divided into four parts, each managed by one of the Allied nations—the USSR, the United States, France, and Britain.

The USSR insisted that for its own protection it needed to keep control over Eastern Europe, which its armies had occupied as it advanced toward Germany. The Soviets aided communist movements in those areas to help them gain power. The western allies viewed this as a sign of aggression, and feared that the USSR wanted to spread communism across the world.

The Truman Doctrine

In 1947, U.S. president Harry Truman proclaimed the Truman Doctrine. It called for the "containment" of communism. By containment Truman meant that the United States and its allies would try to prevent communist revolutions in Europe, Asia, Africa, and South America, and would not allow communist nations to invade their neighbors. By the 1950s, China, North Korea, and many Eastern European countries, including Poland, Czechoslovakia, and Romania, had been converted to communist rule. In addition, the Soviet Union had developed nuclear weapons. The United States and its allies formed the North Atlantic Treaty Organization (NATO) to prevent communism's spread in Europe. A few years later, the communist countries formed the Warsaw Pact, pledging to protect and defend each other. The Cold War was now under way.

After the USSR developed nuclear weapons, they were sometimes paraded through Red Square in Moscow, the capital of the USSR.

One hot spot was Berlin, the former capital of Germany. Because it was the largest and most important German city, it was divided after World War II into four pieces like the rest of the country. As tensions between East and West grew, the U.S. decided to form a government in West Germany that would include West Berlin. The Soviets were upset; they felt that since Berlin was inside East Germany, they should control the whole city. In July of 1948, the USSR cut off shipments of food and supplies to West Berlin. The U.S. and its allies had to fly supplies to the people of West Berlin by airplane and helicopter—an operation known as the Berlin Airlift. The Soviets finally gave in and ended the blockade, but the status of West Berlin would be a major source of hostility between the two sides throughout the Cold War.

West Berlin children cheer a plane bringing supplies during the Berlin airlift in 1948. The communists had sealed off the borders to West Berlin.

Post-Stalin USSR challenges U.S.

In 1953 Stalin died. The new Soviet leader was Nikita Khrushchev. One of his first acts was to condemn the crimes Stalin had committed against the Soviet people. He exposed the cruelty of the labor camps and the party purges, and appeared to take a softer stand toward the United States. Some people began to believe that the Cold War was thawing. These hopes did not last. In 1957, the Russians launched Sputnik, the first space satellite. A few years later they became the first nation to put a man in space. Many Americans feared that Soviet technology might be superior to American technology, and that this might increase the threat of communist domination of the world.

Spying, lying, and hostility

During the last year of Dwight Eisenhower's second term as president, the Cold War heated up. In May 1960, the Soviets shot down a U-2 spy plane above their territory. The Eisenhower administration denied spying on the USSR. But when the captured pilot was produced, the administration had to admit it was lying. Eisenhower refused to promise that the U.S. would stop spying. Two months later, Khrushchev declared the Monroe Doctrine invalid. The Monroe Doctrine was issued by the fifth American president, James Monroe, in 1823. It stated that no nation outside the Western hemisphere would be allowed to interfere in the affairs of nations inside the Western hemisphere. If the Soviets ignored the Monroe Doctrine, they could try to spread communism to countries near the United States.

Castro and the Cuban Revolution

Unstable Cuba

Cuba is a fairly large island about 90 miles (145 kilometers) south of Florida. It was one of the first places settled by Europeans after Christopher Columbus sailed to the Americas in 1492. Until 1898, it was a colony of Spain and produced great amounts of sugar cane. In that year, Cuba won its independence as a result of the Spanish–American War. But even after independence, Cuba was burdened with dishonest and ineffective leaders, and interference in its affairs by the United States.

Cubans often felt they were being mistreated by their large and wealthy neighbor to the north. U.S. citizens and companies owned most of the Cuban sugar, mining, and tourist facilities. Between 1798 and 1962, the U.S. military was sent to Cuba 90 times. Many Cubans began to feel that the U.S. treated their country like a colony. This feeling was strengthened by U.S. support of Fulgencio Batista, a military dictator who ruled the country during the 1940s and 1950s. Batista turned the country into a prime vacation spot for Americans and encouraged American business interests on the island. But life for ordinary people was getting harder as the sugar industry weakened.

Fidel Castro in Havana. Castro became the leader of Cuba in 1959.

Fidel Castro wanted to free Cuba from dictatorship and U.S. domination. Castro was a young student who had been active in radical political movements elsewhere in Latin America. In 1953, he led an attack against the Batista government. It failed and he was imprisoned for nineteen months. In jail he read the works of Karl Marx, but he did not consider himself a communist. After his release, Castro and his followers again attacked the government and spent months in the Sierra Maestra mountains fighting Batista's troops. His movement slowly attracted more support, until finally in 1959 Batista and his family fled Cuba.

Decline in U.S.-Cuba relations

At first many Americans supported Castro and his revolution. They saw Batista as a terrible dictator who oppressed the Cuban people. But Castro's behavior began to disturb American officials, who had provided jets and weapons to Batista's army. Castro executed thousands of people who resisted his regime. He also seized several U.S.-owned businesses and declared them Cuban property.

The Eisenhower administration responded by cutting back Cuba's sugar exports by 80%. The U.S. would buy sugar elsewhere, which would seriously harm Cuba's economy. In February 1962, the U.S. banned other imports from Cuba, including tobacco, molasses, and vegetable products.

To survive economically, Cuba turned to the Soviet Union. In 1959, Soviet advisors started going to Cuba. Although Castro still claimed not to be a communist, he believed his regime had a natural alliance with the USSR. The USSR provided oil and bought Cuba's sugar. Meanwhile, large portions of Cuba's middle class began to abandon their homeland for Florida.

Many Americans believed in the "Domino Theory." This was the belief that if one country became communist, it was likely to support communist movements in neighboring countries. Like a row of dominos knocking each other over, communism would spread from place to place until it took over the world. If communism gained a foothold in Cuba, United States officials were afraid it might spread throughout South America. To prevent this from happening, they decided to oppose the Cuban revolution.

Che Guevara with Nikita Khrushchev, USSR leader, in 1961.

Che Guevara, revolutionary

Castro's most famous ally in his war against Batista was Che Guevara. Guevara was born in Argentina. He studied medicine when he was young, but was more interested in politics and social justice. Guevara joined Castro's rebellion in 1953 and after the revolution, Guevara became Cuba's Minister of Industry. He wrote two books on warfare and revolution and hoped to inspire movements in other Latin American countries. In 1965 he left Cuba to take part in a revolution in Bolivia, where he was captured and shot in 1967.

JFK and the Election of 1960

The contenders

During the United States presidential election campaign of 1960, the situation in Cuba was the most hotly debated issue. The Republican nominee, Richard M. Nixon, had a long history of opposition to communism. As a Senator he was an ally of Joseph McCarthy, who stirred up fears of communism during the early 1950s and held hearings investigating well-known people. Individuals who had been members of the Communist Party lost their jobs and were sometimes put in prison. As Eisenhower's Vice-President, Nixon engaged in a famous debate with Khrushchev, in which the two sides argued over which country produced better consumer goods.

The Democratic Party chose John F. Kennedy to run for president. He was only 44 years old and had little foreign policy experience. He came from Massachusetts, was a World War II hero, and served as a senator for eight years. He was also well-known for his book, *Profiles in Courage,* which won a Pulizer Prize. Historians have also recently learned that Kennedy suffered from a serious illness known as Addison's disease that he kept secret from the public. His illness forced him to wear back braces and to give himself injections. He was often in a lot of pain.

Fear of the USSR's nuclear ability led to drills like this in the Cold War. At a signal, children ducked under their desks and covered their heads. This was thought effective against a nuclear bomb attack.

Memories of Munich

During the election campaign a constant theme was the need to avoid "appeasement." Remembering the Munich Conference in 1938, newspaper editors, politicians, and ordinary Americans felt it was very important to take a strong stand against Khrushchev and communism.

Richard Nixon, from his presidential election debate with John F. Kennedy, October 21, 1960:

"There is only one threat to peace and one threat to freedom—and that is presented by the international communist movement. And therefore if we are to have peace, we must know how to deal with the communists and their leaders. I know Mr. Khrushchev. I also have had the opportunity of knowing and meeting other communist leaders in the world. I believe there are certain principles we must find in dealing with him and his colleagues—principles, if followed, that will keep the peace and that also can extend freedom."

For instance, one of the fiercest campaign issues of 1960 involved the islands of Quemoy and Matsu, near China. The islands were claimed both by Taiwan, an ally of the U.S., and China, a communist nation. Nixon declared that if the Chinese were to take those tiny islands by force, the United States would go to war to defend them. Kennedy at first disagreed with this position. He believed it was better to negotiate with the Chinese, rather than to risk thousands of deaths for two very small islands. But voicing this opinion opened him to harsh criticism. He was accused of being "soft" on communism and of promoting appeasement. From that point on, Kennedy took an aggressive position on all issues related to communism.

Another important election theme in political debates was the so-called "missile gap." After *Sputnik,* many Americans worried that Soviet technology was superior and that the Soviets may have secretly developed more and better nuclear weapons than the U.S. The Eisenhower administration discovered that this was false; by 1961 the United States had 5,000 nuclear warheads and the Soviet Union had only 300. But it could not make this information public without letting the Soviets know the U.S. was spying on them.

John F. Kennedy being sworn in as president on January 20, 1961. Richard Nixon is at the far right.

Therefore, many Americans continued to believe that the United States needed to quickly develop more nuclear weapons to catch up with the Soviets. There was a great deal of fear and anxiety in the U.S. at this time. Throughout the 1950s, Americans prepared for the possibility of nuclear war. Schoolchildren practiced drills in case of an attack, and some people even built bomb shelters, rooms with super-strong walls, in their basements.

The presidential election was extremely close, but Kennedy won. In his Inaugural Address he famously said, "Ask not what your country can do for you, ask what you can do for your country." He urged Americans to make the world a better place through programs like the Peace Corps. But most of his address focused on the struggle between liberal democracy and communism. Kennedy promised that the United States would "pay any price, bear any burden, meet any hardship, support any friend, oppose any foe" to make sure liberty triumphed.

Disaster at the Bay of Pigs

Handed-down invasion plan

In 1960, before the election, the Central Intelligence Agency (CIA) began secretly planning to help rebels invade Cuba and overthrow Castro's regime. Eisenhower knew of the plans, but had not given final approval for an invasion. Nixon hoped the CIA would do something immediately before the election that might help him beat Kennedy. Meanwhile, the CIA helped arm and train several thousand Cuban exiles in Guatemala. It promised them that the U.S. military would provide support when they landed in Cuba.

When he became president, Kennedy was asked to approve this plan. He felt it would be a mistake to cancel an operation begun by the previous administration, so he agreed to allow the invasion to take place. He refused, however, to involve American troops, or to support the invasion with as much U.S. air power as the CIA wanted. The result was a disaster.

On April 17, 1961, the rebels landed at the Bay of Pigs on the south side of Cuba. Two United States fighters disguised as Cuban jets destroyed part of the Cuban air force to give the rebels time to invade the island. But Kennedy had been misled by the CIA. The rebels were quickly overwhelmed by Castro's forces when they landed. The support they expected to receive from the Cuban people never showed up. When it became clear that the invasion was in trouble, Kennedy refused to call in air strikes to save the invasion. Of the 1,400 invaders, 114 were killed and 1,189 were captured.

The United States naval base at Guantanomo Bay, Cuba. The CIA hoped President Kennedy would have these troops support the Bay of Pigs invasion.

Consequences of failure

The Bay of Pigs failure was a tremendous embarrassment for Kennedy. It strengthened the image many people held of him as young, inexperienced, and soft on communism. Republicans across the country, and many Democrats too, attacked him for missing a golden opportunity to remove Castro from power. Most importantly, Khrushchev interpreted Kennedy's refusal to commit troops and planes as a sign of weakness. He resolved to press the American leader to make the Soviet Union look stronger to the world.

After the attempted invasion, Castro began to describe his movement as a "socialist" revolution. Anger against the United States spread around the world in reaction to the attempted invasion, and citizens in several countries threw stones at U.S. embassies. The Soviets tried to use the Bay of Pigs incident to show the world that communism was the wave of the future and that capitalism was doomed.

Operation Mongoose

Because of this humiliation, the Kennedy administration now believed they had to get tough with Castro and with the Soviet Union. One project inspired by the Bay of Pigs failure was "Operation Mongoose." This was a CIA plan, first launched in November 1961, to weaken the Cuban government through sabotage. If a civil war were to break out in Cuba, the U.S was prepared to come and take part to defeat Castro.

Allan Dulles, CIA Director, on Kennedy's handling of the Bay of Pigs:

"I should have realized that, if he had no enthusiasm about the idea in the first place, he would drop it at the first opportunity rather than do the things necessary to make it succeed."

The government gathered Cuban exiles in Miami, Florida, to train for a possible invasion. The CIA also attempted to assassinate Castro and his brother Raul by a variety of methods, such as poisoning their cigars. They even tried to get Mafia members to find ways to kill the Castros, but all their efforts failed.

Sparring in Vienna and Berlin

The leaders meet

On June 3 and 4, 1961, Kennedy and Khrushchev held their first summit meeting in Vienna, Austria. A summit is a face-to-face talk between the highest officials of two or more governments. It was a way for the leaders of the U.S. and the Soviet Union to build trust and confidence in each other by developing a personal relationship.

Kennedy hoped that the summit would provide a chance to reduce the tensions between the two sides that had been building over the last few years. Khrushchev, however, tried to press Kennedy for concessions and to build prestige for the USSR. He accused the United States of supporting cruel dictators like Batista and Spain's Francisco Franco. He demanded that Berlin— still divided into Soviet and Western sectors—be united with East Germany. Khrushchev decided that Kennedy's behavior during the Bay of Pigs proved he was not a strong and determined leader. At the end of the meeting he suggested that if the situation in Berlin was not resolved, war between the two sides might be possible.

Soviet and U.S. tanks face each other at "Checkpoint Charlie" in Berlin on October 28, 1961. The world came close to war on this day, before the two generals in charge pulled back their forces.

The meeting in Vienna changed Kennedy's attitude toward the Soviet Union. He was no longer hopeful of easing the hostility on each side and believed he would have to be tougher towards Khrushchev.

The Berlin Wall

In the fall of 1961, the status of Berlin became a big issue. Kennedy again warned the Soviets that any attempt to attack West Berlin would mean nuclear war. The Soviets had a problem. Economic troubles were causing many East Germans to leave for West Germany. This greatly embarrassed the communist governments, since it suggested that workers were worse off under communist rule. The East German response in October was to build a giant wall across the city of Berlin, preventing anyone from leaving or entering the East without special permission. In addition, barbed wire was placed along the border between East and West Germany, to stop people from going to the West.

The "missile gap" unmasked

Kennedy decided to publicize the fact that the United States had far more nuclear weapons than the USSR, in an attempt to convince the Soviets that more aggression would be a mistake. This was the opposite of what Kennedy had repeatedly said during the presidential election. A Soviet defector passed along information showing that the Soviets only possessed 25 intercontinental ballistic missiles (ICBMs) capable of striking the United States. The U.S., on the other hand, had several hundred ICBMs. If there was a missile gap, it was in U.S. superiority to the Soviets, not the other way around. When one of Kennedy's aides made this information public, it was another embarrassment for Khrushchev. It seemed to reveal to the world Soviet military weakness, at least in comparison to the United States.

Nuclear testing

Khrushchev responded to this news by resuming nuclear tests. On October 30, the largest explosion in human history took place on an island in the Arctic Ocean. The bomb was several hundred times bigger than those the U.S. dropped on Japan during World War II. The flash of light it gave off could be seen 667 miles (1,000 kilometers) away. Khrushchev was heard saying, "Let this device hang over the heads of the capitalists, like a sword of Damocles." Within a few months, the U.S. would also resume nuclear tests. The Cold War was hotter than ever.

Kennedy and Kruschev talk at the Vienna summit. Kruschev's impression after this meeting was that Kennedy was not a strong leader.

Arming Cuba

Krushchev's proposal

The Kremlin was a large castle in Moscow where the leaders of the Soviet government had their offices. At a Kremlin meeting in May 1962, Khrushchev first proposed putting missiles in Cuba. He had three major reasons for doing this. First, he needed to do something in response to the damaging news about United States nuclear superiority. Placing missiles close to the United States would make the balance of power more equal. The second reason was to help defend the Cuban revolution. Cuba had moved closer and closer toward communism, and as it did, the demands by some Americans to overthrow the regime grew louder. Castro himself believed the U.S. was planning to invade. With nuclear weapons in Cuba, Khrushchev knew the U.S would not risk an invasion—that might lead to nuclear war. He was hoping that he could secretly install the weapons without the U.S. realizing it. Once the missiles were in place, he thought Kennedy would have no choice but to accept them. Finally, Khrushchev was angry that the U.S. had placed nuclear weapons in one of the Soviet Union's neighbors, Turkey.

Castro asks for protection

Operation Mongoose became active in late 1961. As U.S. hostility became clear, Castro was desperate for Soviet support. He asked for a Soviet promise to defend Cuba in case of invasion, but Khrushchev decided to be even bolder. On May 21, 1962, Khrushchev presented a plan to place missiles in Cuba. Some Soviet leaders questioned the idea, but Khrushchev overcame their opposition. In July he began secretly shipping missiles, troops, airplanes, and other weapons to Cuba. The weapons were carefully hidden, so that even when U.S. spy planes flew overhead, they could not tell what the ships were carrying.

A photo of the Kremlin in the Red Square in Moscow.

The U.S. position

The first shipments of missiles left the USSR in July, and almost immediately rumors spread in the U.S. that missiles had been placed in Cuba. Cuban refugees escaping to Miami reported seeing strange military developments before they left. But the Kennedy administration felt it was unlikely that the Soviets would do anything so foolish. In a major speech in September 1962, Kennedy declared that there was no reason to believe Soviet missiles were in Cuba, but if that ever happened, the United States would use force to remove them. If Cuba were to "become an offensive military base of significant capacity for the Soviet Union, then this country would do whatever must be done to protect its own security and that of its allies."

American public opinion, however, grew increasingly anxious and hostile. Politicians of both parties, and newspapers and magazines of all types, felt Kennedy was not doing enough about the threat in Cuba, and urged an invasion. The CIA continued Operation Mongoose, but planning went slowly. The CIA hoped Castro would do something that would justify an invasion or let the U.S. support a rebellion. But Castro, knowing that Soviet missiles to protect him were coming, did not give the U.S. the chance.

The threat installed

Eventually, 36 medium-range missiles—which could strike Texas—and 24 intermediate-range missiles—which could reach Seattle—were sent to Cuba. By the time the United States learned about the missiles, 42,000 Soviet troops were stationed in Cuba and 80 cruise missiles defended the island from a U.S. attack. A U.S. invasion would result in a bloody and terrible battle.

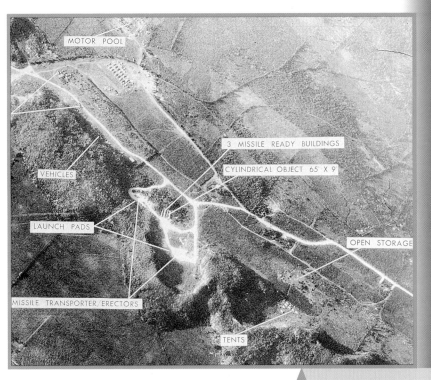

A United States spy plane photgraph of the Cuban missile sites. Construction of the missile sites happened fairly rapidly after Kruschev made the decision to place missiles in Cuba.

Ex-Comm

The U.S. finds out

Throughout 1962, U-2 spy planes took photographs of Cuban ships, planes, military bases, and possible missile sites. A U-2 is a giant plane with an 80-foot (24-meter) wing span. It can fly more than 70,000 feet (21,336 meters) above the ground and has cameras attached to its underside. Nothing the U-2 planes recorded during early autumn of 1962 showed evidence of forbidden weapons. Suddenly on October 15, new spy pictures showed that Soviet missile installations had been built in the western part of Cuba.

A CIA official named Ray Cline brought the pictures directly to the president. Kennedy quietly informed his closest advisors, but tried not to let people know anything was wrong. The next day Kennedy formed what would later be known as the "Executive Committee of the United States Security Council," or Ex-Comm for short. This was a group of his closest and most talented advisors on foreign policy issues. They would help Kennedy make the important decisions of the next two weeks. Kennedy felt that the Bay of Pigs might have been avoided if he had had a chance to hear several different arguments and points of view. The group met in secret, because the government did not want the Soviets or the American people to know what they had learned.

Advisors Theodore Sorensen, McGeorge Bundy, Robert Kennedy, and Kenneth O'Donnell outside President Kennedy's office.

Ex-Comm members

Fourteen people were regular participants in Ex-Comm meetings. The most important members were Robert Kennedy, the Attorney General, who was also Kennedy's brother; Lyndon B. Johnson, the Vice-President; Dean Rusk, the Secretary of State; and Robert McNamara, the Secretary of Defense. Other participants had less important jobs, but were valuable for their intelligence and experience. Llewelyn Thompson was a former ambassador to the USSR and most likely knew more about the Soviet Union than anyone else in the administration. McGeorge Bundy, the National Security Advisor, was one of the smartest men in the administration; Theodore Sorenson, Kennedy's Special Counsel, had worked for the president for many years; and George Ball, the Under-Secretary of State, was a valuable advisor. Dean Acheson was a former Secretary of State who was involved in the first steps of the Cold War when Harry Truman was president.

The other members of Ex-Comm were Roswell Gilpatric, McNamara's deputy; Douglas Dillon, the Secretary of the Treasury; General Maxwell Taylor, Chairman of the Joint Chiefs of Staff; John McCone, head of the CIA; and two other state department officials, U. Alexis Johnson, and Edwin Martin. Several other officials occasionally visited Ex-Comm meetings, but were not regular members.

An Ex-Comm meeting. President Kennedy sits in the middle of the table on the opposite side.

Meeting in secret

Ex-Comm was small enough that it could meet in secret. The members could be trusted not to leak information to the media, which might ruin their plans. Once several members of Ex-Comm got into a car and sneaked into the back entrance of the White House. If several limousines had arrived at the front door all at once, reporters would know something important was happening.

Ex-Comm was also large enough that many different opinions were represented. No one person dominated the discussions. Historians know a great deal about the Ex-Comm meetings thanks to tape recorders that were running in the rooms where they met. Those recordings offer a fascinating glimpse into how decisions were made in moments of intense pressure.

Invasion vs. Blockade

First reaction

During the first 24 hours after the crisis began, most members of Ex-Comm were prepared to invade Cuba right away. Robert Kennedy later wrote that without more time to decide, they probably would have begun a war. Dean Acheson, for instance, supported an immediate strike against the missiles, even though he knew the Soviets would respond by attacking U.S. targets in Europe, and the crisis then might spiral out of control. The administration was still shocked and frightened, and its first reaction was to use military force.

Second thoughts

The next day, Wednesday, October 17, 1962, more careful opinions emerged. George Ball was the first Ex-Comm member to argue against invasion. He felt that an unprompted attack would resemble the Japanese one on the U.S. at Pearl Harbor, Hawaii, in 1941, which brought the United States into World War II. On October 18, Robert Kennedy seconded this position. "My brother is not going to be the Tojo of the 1960s," he said. (Tojo was the Japanese leader who ordered the attack on Pearl Harbor.) He raised moral questions, asking what kind of nation the U.S. was and whether it was willing to risk thousands of Cuban, Soviet, and American lives. He believed the U.S. would damage its position in the world if it attacked another country without warning.

Robert Kennedy anxiously paces at another Ex-Comm meeting. President Kennedy is second from the right.

Ball and Robert Kennedy instead argued for a naval blockade of Cuba. Soon other members of Ex-Comm, including Ted Sorenson and Robert McNamara, agreed with them. American naval vessels would form a circle around Cuba and prevent any ship carrying military equipment from reaching the island until the missiles were removed. Such an idea was not entirely new. Many politicians had called for a blockade even before the existence of Soviet missiles was discovered, and polls showed that the public favored a blockade over a war.

The president's decision

Some of the Ex-Comm members could not make up their minds. McGeorge Bundy, for example, argued first for an invasion, then for a blockade, then again for an invasion. He changed his mind almost daily. By Thursday, October 18, however, the president was leaning toward a blockade over an invasion. A blockade would give the Soviets a chance to back down and possibly avoid armed conflict.

The President talks with his advisors outside the White House. Although choosing what to do was ultimately up to President Kennedy, hearing all his advisors' opinions helped strengthen his final decision.

Within Ex-Comm, a few people still called for air strikes, but the majority favored a blockade. But pressure remained to take stronger action. On October 19, Kennedy met with the Joint Chiefs of Staff—the heads of the different military branches (Army, Navy, Air Force, and Marines). They all urged an invasion, and claimed that anything else would simply repeat the appeasement of the Munich Agreement. But to Kennedy, the real issue was avoiding a tragedy: "Now, the question really is to what action we take which lessens the chances of a nuclear exchange, which is obviously the final failure—that's obvious to us—and at the same time, maintain some degree of solidarity with our allies," he said.

Even as they struggled to find a peaceful solution to the crisis, government officials quietly began the largest increase of U.S. military forces since World War II. Thousands of troops and equipment were assembled in south Florida, Puerto Rico, and Guantanamo Bay, Cuba, where the U.S. has a naval base. Kennedy wanted to be ready for anything that might happen.

More than a brother

Robert F. Kennedy was born in 1925 in Massachusetts. After World War II, he went to law school, then managed his brother John's Senate campaign in 1952. He also ran Kennedy's presidential campaign in 1960. His grateful brother named him Attorney General, or head of the Justice Department. As Attorney General, Robert F. Kennedy was involved in the civil rights struggle. He sent troops to the South to defend the rights of blacks to vote and attend universities. He also struggled to eliminate organized crime. In 1964, he resigned as Attorney General and was elected to the Senate. In 1968 he ran for president and probably had a good chance of being elected. He pledged among other things to end the war in Vietnam as quickly as possible. But while giving a speech in California after a campaign victory on June 5, 1968, Robert F. Kennedy was shot and killed by a man named Sirhan Sirhan.

Going Public

On October 21, 1962, former president Dwight Eisenhower helped support Kennedy's plan by urging Republicans not to talk too much about Cuba. With an election coming up in November, Republican candidates were eager to criticize the president's policies. Eisenhower helped make sure that the U.S. looked united when the next day Kennedy announced his plan for a blockade.

Kennedy speaks to America

On Monday, October 22, Kennedy spoke to the nation for about seventeen minutes on television. He revealed the presence of missiles in Cuba "capable of striking Washington, D.C., the Panama Canal, Mexico City, or any other city in the southeastern United States, in central America, or in the Caribbean area." He stressed that the Soviets had

An American family watches President Kennedy speak to the nation about the Soviet missiles in Cuba.

repeatedly lied in promising the U.S. that they would not place weapons in Cuba. He then described the U.S. plan to blockade the island until the missiles were removed. "To halt this offensive buildup, a strict quarantine on all offensive military equipment under shipment to Cuba is being initiated. All ships of any kind bound for Cuba from whatever nation or port will, if found to contain cargoes of offensive weapons, be turned back."

Kennedy used the word "quarantine" rather than "blockade" to describe the naval action. The word quarantine was meant to remind people of a speech Franklin D. Roosevelt made as president in 1937. Roosevelt called for "peace-loving nations" to "quarantine the aggressors," which at that time referred to Germany and Japan. By comparing Cuba and the Soviet Union to Nazi Germany and Imperial Japan, Kennedy wanted to make the U.S. blockade seem like a defensive action. In fact, a blockade is usually considered an act of war in international law, since it can deny people the goods they need to survive. Calling the blockade a quarantine helped make the Soviets look like the aggressors.

At the same time, Kennedy's speech was very aggressive. He claimed that it was better to risk nuclear war than surrender to the spread of communism. He discouraged any "hostile move" against "the brave people of West Berlin." Kennedy ended his speech by preparing Americans for a long struggle: "Many months of sacrifice and self-discipline lie ahead...Our goal is not the victory of might, but the vindication of right."

This photo shows Soviet missile sites being constructed at San Cristobal, Cuba.

Public opinion

The reaction to Kennedy's speech was almost entirely positive. The White House received 4,000 telegrams after the address, and almost all of them approved of Kennedy's plan. A minority of "hawks" still felt an immediate invasion was necessary, but their voices were drowned out by supporters of the president. There were few protesters on college campuses critical of the blockade, which was different from a few years later when the U.S. went to war in Vietnam. Politicians, newspaper editors, and ordinary citizens all argued that it was important to avoid another Munich Agreement. With this one speech to the nation, Kennedy had erased memories of the Bay of Pigs and other foreign policy mistakes, and transformed himself in the eyes of many into a capable leader.

President Kennedy, TV star

Kennedy was the first president to make frequent use of television. In fact, without it he might not have been elected in the first place. Americans began buying TVs for their homes in 1948, but 1960 was the first year that presidential debates were shown on television. Under the hot TV lights Richard Nixon looked tired, uncomfortable, and sweaty. Kennedy, on the other hand, was handsome and relaxed, and that probably helped him win the election.

Diplomacy

Because a blockade could be seen as an act of war, it was very important for the U.S. government to win support from the international community. Two organizations were especially vital, the United Nations (UN) and the Organization of American States (OAS).

The OAS meeting in New York.

The Americas

The OAS met the day after Kennedy's speech. There were 21 republics in North and South America. A two-thirds majority, or fourteen votes, would be needed to approve the blockade. Dean Rusk, the Secretary of State, made the presentation for the United States. After an afternoon of discussion, the council voted 19 to 0 to support the blockade. Only one country, Uruguay, did not vote, because a bad connection prevented its ambassador from reaching his superiors on the telephone.

This show of cooperation among the nations of the western hemisphere made the Soviet government take notice. It also made people recall the claim in the Monroe Doctrine that nations in the eastern hemisphere should not interfere in the affairs of the western hemisphere.

World opinion

Next the U.S. had to win over the UN, where the U.S. ambassador in charge of diplomacy was Adlai Stevenson. Stevenson had run for president twice, losing each time to Eisenhower. He was one of the most respected Democrats in the country. He was often critical, however, of anti-communism, and believed that Kennedy's blockade was a dangerous and irresponsible idea. Therefore, relations between Kennedy and Stevenson were not very good. Nonetheless, it was Stevenson's job to convince the United Nations to endorse the blockade.

The secretary-general, or leader, of the United Nations was a man named U Thant. Thant, from Burma, was accepted by both sides as a fair negotiator. He played an important role in making sure the quarrel did not get out of control, and tried to keep the two sides talking to each other. On October 24, 1962, Thant proposed a cooling-off period of a few weeks, during which both the quarantine and the Soviet arms shipments would be stopped. The Kennedy administration did not like this idea, since it would allow the Soviets to continue building missile sites in Cuba with nuclear material that had already arrived. The president rejected the proposal, but suggested an alternative. If the Soviets would stay out of the blockade zone, the U.S. would take part in talks and stall for time.

Although Khrushchev had already admitted to American officials that missiles were in Cuba, the Soviet ambassador to the UN, Valerian Zorin, still claimed there were not. Zorin let himself get drawn into a confrontation with Stevenson at a UN Security Council meeting that embarrassed the USSR. As millions of people in the U.S. and around the world watched on television, Stevenson presented detailed images of the missile sites, proving that the Soviet denials were false. Thanks to this dramatic display, the U.S. was able to win support for its blockade from the UN, and the USSR's image was hurt in world public opinion.

Adlai Stevenson, U.S. ambassador to the UN, shows evidence of missiles in Cuba to the UN Security Council.

Showdown at UN

From the exchange between Adlai Stevenson and Valerian Zorin at the United Nations, October 25, 1962:

Stevenson: *"Do you, Ambassador Zorin, deny that the USSR has placed and is placing medium and intermediate range missiles and sites in Cuba? Yes or no? Don't wait for the translation, yes or no?"*

Zorin: *"I am not in an American courtroom, sir, and therefore I do not wish to answer a question that is put to me in a fashion in which a prosecutor puts questions."*

Stevenson: *"You are in the courtroom of world opinion right now and you can answer yes or no... I am prepared to wait for my answer until hell freezes over, if that is your decision. And I am also prepared to present the evidence in this room."*

Stevenson then presented spy photographs showing the missile sites.

Eyeball to Eyeball

The blockade went into effect 39 hours after Kennedy's speech, on Wednesday October 24, 1962. The delay was meant to give Khrushchev time to think over the consequences of ignoring the quarantine. The line of quarantine was first set at 800 miles (1287 kilometers) from the Cuban shore, then moved in to 500 miles (805 kilometers), and then even closer as the U.S. stalled for time. All ships entering the quarantined area would be boarded and searched by U.S. naval vessels. The U.S. used 180 ships to form the blockade, which was overseen by the Secretary of Defense, Robert McNamara. To help win international support, the quarantine did not apply to medical supplies, food, or oil. Kennedy did not want to appear to be punishing ordinary Cuban men, women, and children.

Enforcing the blockade

During the night of Tuesday, October 24, several Soviet ships heading for Cuba turned back, including the *Poltava,* which carried twenty nuclear warheads. The Soviets did not want this valuable cargo to fall into American hands. But two ships, the *Yuri Gagarin* and the *Komiles,* kept going. By Wednesday morning the vessels, defended by Soviet submarines, were nearing the quarantine line. Khrushchev had pledged that Soviet submarines would sink U.S. ships if they enforced the blockade. Ex-Comm believed that a confrontation was only moments away. A naval destroyer, the *Essex,* was ordered to drop depth charges until the submarines surfaced and identified themselves. Suddenly, at 10:32 a.m., the CIA learned that the Soviet ships had turned around. Khrushchev did not want to challenge the quarantine with ships carrying nuclear cargo. Dean Rusk said to an Ex-Comm colleague, "We're eyeball to eyeball, and I think the other fellow just blinked."

President Kennedy signs the quarantine proclamation which announced that the U.S. would board and search ships nearing Cuba.

But the crisis was far from over. To get the Soviets to remove the missiles from Cuba entirely, Kennedy felt he needed to increase the pressure. On Friday, October 26, he enforced the blockade for the first time against another country. To avoid more tension, the administration specifically chose a non-Soviet ship for the first inspection. At 7:00 that morning the destroyer *Joseph P. Kennedy Jr.,* named after Kennedy's father, ordered a freighter named the *Marcula* to stop. The *Marcula* was a Lebanese-owned ship carrying sulfur, newsprint rolls, trucks, and spare parts. A group of U.S. seamen boarded the ship and briefly searched it. Once they were certain it did not carry any weapons, it was allowed to continue on to Cuba.

The John R. Pierce, *one of two destroyers that intercepted the* Marcula.

Increased tensions in Cuba

Meanwhile in Cuba, Soviet technicians hurried to put the missiles together. Some Ex-Comm members argued that they should be destroyed before they were ready to fire, which could happen within hours. Kennedy responded however by increasing the number of U-2 and other spy planes flying over Cuba, so that he could keep an eye on the missiles. Castro gave his soldiers permission to shoot down U.S. planes flying over Cuba, which Khrushchev later described as a mistake: "It became clear to us that Fidel totally failed to understand our purpose...We had installed the missiles not for the purpose of attacking the United States, but to keep the United States from attacking Cuba."

The Jupiters

At an Ex-Comm meeting on Friday October 27, 1962, Adlai Stevenson forecasted that the Soviets would remove the Cuban missiles, but only on two conditions. The U.S. would have to promise not to invade Cuba, and it would have to remove its nuclear weapons from Turkey. Many members of Ex-Comm refused to consider such a trade-off, arguing that the U.S. missiles were "defensive" while the Soviet ones were "offensive." This was a common argument made by each side, because they saw their opponent as the aggressor. The Soviets believed their missiles were in Cuba to defend Castro from a U.S. invasion, and the U.S. believed it had missiles in Turkey to prevent a Soviet takeover of that country.

A Polaris submarine. Polaris submarines carry nuclear missiles.

U.S. missiles near USSR

Turkey was the only member of NATO that directly bordered the Soviet Union. Turkey and Russia fought numerous wars during the nineteenth and twentieth centuries, partly because Russia's only passage to the sea lay through the Dardanelles strait, which Turkey controlled. The Turks were concerned by the new power of the Soviet Union. Khrushchev had declared in the 1950s, "If war breaks out, Turkey would not last one day." The Turks requested that nuclear missiles be installed as a defense against Soviet invasion. Since the U.S. was placing weapons in Britain and Italy, it decided to place fifteen Jupiter missiles in Turkey as well.

U.S. officials under the Eisenhower administration were never very happy with this idea. Not only were they threatening the Soviets with missiles close to their territory, but the weapons themselves were not very effective. The Jupiters were rather old nuclear devices. They were stored above ground, rather than in underground storage installations called silos, so in case of a war they could easily be located and destroyed by enemy airplanes. They could also be damaged by the weather. The Jupiters were so out of date some U.S. officials weren't sure they would fly in the right direction.

Eisenhower would have preferred to defend Turkey with Polaris submarines. But the Turks insisted that missiles were necessary to their security and the U.S. did not want to disappoint an ally. The Kennedy administration also felt uncomfortable about the Jupiters, but it went ahead with the final installation in early March 1962. By this time, the missiles had been handed over to the Turks, although the warheads remained in U.S. control.

Soviet fears

To the Soviets it seemed rather hypocritical that Americans were so disturbed by the Cuban missiles when U.S. missiles were pointed at Soviet people in a neighboring country. Even though they knew the missiles were not very dangerous, they did not like the idea of having them so close. Khrushchev himself had a summer home in Sochi, only miles from the Jupiters. He claimed he could see them with binoculars across the Black Sea. The Soviets were especially frightened that the Turkish military might be able to launch a nuclear attack without the U.S. knowing about it. In reality, that was impossible since U.S. soldiers still controlled the warheads. Along with the Turkish missiles, bombs pointed at Soviet cities were located in other European countries, too.

A Jupiter missile. Because Turkey feared a Soviet attack, the U.S. placed Jupiters in Turkey although they were out of date.

One of the first people to call publicly for eliminating missiles in both Cuba and Turkey as a kind of trade was a well-known newspaper columnist named Walter Lippmann. Writing in his column in the *Washington Post*, Lippmann argued that the situations in both countries were rather similar. If the U.S. wanted the Cuban missiles removed, it would have to be willing to take the Jupiters out of Turkey. "The two bases could be eliminated without altering the world balance of power," he wrote. When the Soviets read Lippmann's column, they began to believe that a compromise would be possible.

Editorial from the *Philadelphia Inquirer* October 24, 1962 on the difference between Turkish and Cuban missiles.

"The Soviets, by Khrushchev's own admission, are out to conquer the world. Soviet missile bases are for that purpose. They are for aggression and enslavement. United States missile bases at home and abroad are for the defense of freedom. They are to protect mankind against the menacing evil of communist tyranny [rule]."

A Possible Solution

Signs of an opening

On Friday afternoon several signs appeared that the Soviets were willing to make a deal. At 1:30 p.m. John Scali, a reporter for the ABC television network, got a call from Alexander Fomin. Fomin was known to be an important person in the Soviet intelligence service, the KGB. He invited Scali to lunch at a nearby hotel. Fomin was concerned that events were getting out of control, and he suggested that Khrushchev might be willing to remove the missiles from Cuba in return for a U.S. pledge not to invade the island. As a journalist, Scali could not speak for the U.S. government, but passed the news on to the White House.

U Thant was the UN Secretary General in 1960. The U.S. worked actively within the UN during the Crisis.

At almost the same time, U Thant made a similar proposal to Adlai Stevenson. Kennedy was not sure at first whether the proposal was an actual offer from the Soviet government, or just a plan thought up by U Thant. At about 4:00 that afternoon, Kennedy received a letter from Khrushchev. After a long defense of Soviet policy and complaints about the blockade and U.S. hostility to the Cuban revolution, Khrushchev made Kennedy an offer: "Let us therefore show statesmanlike wisdom. I propose: we, for our part, will declare that our ships bound for Cuba will not carry any kind of armaments [weapons]. You would declare that the United States will not invade Cuba with its forces and will not support any kind of forces that might intend to carry out an invasion of Cuba."

This was still unacceptable to the Kennedy administration, since Khrushchev did not mention removing the missiles already in Cuba. Still, some members of Ex-Comm thought they saw the beginnings of a solution, and a willingness by Khrushchev to resolve the dispute. Ex-Comm members read the letter over and over, trying to figure out what Khrushchev intended to do and trying to decide whether they could trust him.

President Kennedy and U.S. generals with missiles during the Crisis. Would they have to fire the missiles?

Khrushchev's second message

The next day Khrushchev sent another message to Kennedy, this time via radio. After sleeping on the problem he made a tougher offer. He now objected to the missiles in Turkey and argued that Soviets had the same fears regarding their own security that Americans now felt with missiles in Cuba. "Do you believe that you have the right to demand security for your country and the removal of such weapons that you call offensive, but do not accord the same right to us?" He proposed a kind of missile swap: the Soviet Union would remove its weapons from Cuba and the United States would pull the Jupiters out of Turkey. The Soviets would pledge not to invade Turkey and the U.S. would promise not to attack Cuba.

Ex-Comm was disturbed that Khrushchev had changed his proposal overnight, and they did not want to deal with the Turkish question or engage in any kind of missile swap. They believed that the situation in Cuba was a separate issue that involved only the nations of the western hemisphere. To bring the situation in Europe into the dispute would make it seem as if the administration was not taking a hard stand against the Soviets over Cuba. McGeorge Bundy urged the president to ignore this second message and instead reply to Khrushchev's first letter as if he had never sent the new one.

New Tensions

The heads of the United States military continued to argue that the government should stop negotiating and attack Cuba immediately. This position suddenly gained great support when officials learned that a U-2 spy plane had been shot down over Cuba, and its pilot had been killed.

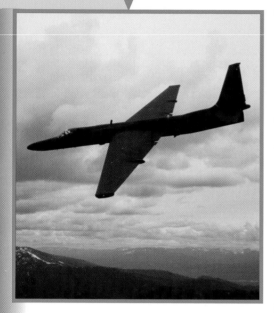

A U-2 spy plane.

The plane's pilot, Major Rudolph Anderson, had taken photographs less than two weeks earlier that proved the existence of the Cuban missiles. When his plane was spotted over eastern Cuba, Soviet soldiers shot it down without receiving permission from Moscow. Khrushchev was furious at this action and so were many Cuban officials. They knew it might lead to war.

Even more upset were the members of Ex-Comm. Llewellyn Thompson urged Kennedy to destroy a Soviet surface-to-air (SAM) missile site immediately, without any warning or explanation. Other officials also felt some military response was necessary and suggested planning an attack for the next week. Kennedy rejected this advice and decided to seek a peaceful resolution to the crisis by responding to Khrushchev's earlier offers.

The "Trollope ploy"

Kennedy wrote a public letter to the Soviet Chairman agreeing to call off the quarantine and to not invade Cuba if the missiles were removed. As Bundy had suggested, he did not refer to the Jupiters or to Khrushchev's Saturday morning message. This became known as the "Trollope ploy" after a nineteenth-century novelist whose characters sometimes heard what they wanted to hear and ignored everything else. Three times Kennedy referred to "your letter of October 26" to emphasize that he was responding to that offer. Kennedy did not want

---

Robert Kennedy on Ex-Comm's reaction to the loss of the U-2 and Kennedy's calming influence, from his book *Thirteen Days*:

"At first, there was almost unanimous agreement that we had to attack early the next morning with bombers and fighters and destroy the SAM sites. But again the President pulled everyone back. 'It isn't the first step that concerns me,' he said, 'but both sides escalating to the fourth and fifth step—and we don't go to the sixth because there is no one around to do so. We must remind ourselves we are embarking on a very hazardous course'."

any public sign that he was willing to make a deal over the Jupiters, so he simply ignored that demand. The most he would say was that if the crisis could be resolved, it "would enable us to work toward a more general arrangement regarding 'other armaments,' as proposed in your second letter..." Saturday afternoon Robert Kennedy personally delivered the letter to Anatoly Dobrynin, the Soviet ambassador to the U.S.

When Robert Kennedy met with Dobrynin, he was both forceful and yielding. On the one hand, he threatened the use of force if another plane was downed in Cuba, or if the Soviets did not respond to the U.S. offer right away. But he also suggested that the Turkish missiles would be removed, although that part of the deal had to remain secret. He said that Turkey was a member of NATO and the president could not make a decision like that on his own without consulting U.S. allies. Dobrynin also knew that Kennedy's political position would be harmed if the public knew he had swapped missiles. After Robert Kennedy left, Dobrynin wrote a message to Khrushchev, telling him about the offer.

President Kennedy meets with Soviet diplomats during the Cuban Missile Crisis.

Communication delays

By making the letter to Khrushchev public, the administration hoped to speed up the communication process. They had been very frustrated at the amount of time it took for letters to be wired from the USSR to U.S. officials, who then had to translate the documents into English. Khrushchev's first letter on Friday, for instance, had taken eight hours to reach Ex-Comm members. By then it was too late to respond that day. The next morning they had received another letter from Khrushchev changing his position: he now wanted the Jupiters removed. Clearly, more delay would have risked dangerous miscommunication.

One result: the hotline

After the Cuban Missile Crisis was over, leaders on both sides realized they needed to get a better communication system. They installed red phones that became famous as "the hotline," a direct line between the U.S. President and the Soviet Chairman. In case of future emergencies, they would be able to avoid some of the frustration and danger that came with the delay in wiring letters.

The Secret Missile Swap

To the edge

President Kennedy did not much expect that the Soviets would accept the proposal his brother delivered to Dobrynin. On Saturday evening, he began calling up Air Force reserve squadrons in case of another attack on a U.S. plane. Robert McNamara and other Ex-Comm members felt war was highly likely and Bundy later reported that an invasion was scheduled for the following Tuesday.

On Sunday morning, October 28, 1962, Khrushchev wrote another letter to Kennedy. His tone was very different from his previous communications. He no longer scolded the U.S. for aggressive or dangerous behavior. Instead he said he understood that the missiles in Cuba made Americans uneasy. He wrote that "the Soviet Government...has issued a new order to dismantle the weapons which you describe as offensive, and to crate and return them to the Soviet Union." United Nations inspectors would oversee this work and make sure all the weapons were removed.

A mixed reaction

Ex-Comm was thrilled. Kennedy warned them not to celebrate too much, since boasting of victory would embarrass Khrushchev. Still, Kennedy was happy that the crisis had been resolved without making him appear soft on communism. But for all the happiness in Washington, many people were not satisfied with the settlement. In the Soviet Union, citizens were shocked that no public deal had been reached to remove the Jupiters from Turkey. Many felt that their leaders had misled them and were not looking out for their interests. Cuba's

The Soviet ship Divinogorsk carries missiles away from Cuba after the crisis is over.

Castro was furious and felt Khrushchev had betrayed him. Soviet leaders were afraid that in his anger, Castro would shoot down another U.S. plane and start a war. The leaders of the U.S. military believed it was a mistake to leave Castro in power. They told Kennedy, "It's the greatest defeat in our history, Mr. President...We should invade today!"

The Cuban missiles began to be removed on Sunday. Khrushchev had to urge Castro not to block the UN inspections, which could cause the deal to fall apart. The Soviets sent an official to assure the Cubans that the U.S. had promised not to invade Cuba and that if it did the Soviet Union would defend them.

In the following weeks, Soviet ships loaded up the missiles and carried them back to the USSR. By November 7, the CIA announced that this process was under way and would soon be complete. On November 20, 1962, Kennedy lifted the blockade around Cuba and ordered the military to stand down.

MISSILE READY TENT FOUNDATIONS (TENTS REMOVED)

ABANDONED LAUNCH POSITION

Photos like this showed that the Soviets had removed their missiles from Cuba.

Removing the Jupiters

Meanwhile, Kennedy had secretly promised Khrushchev that the Jupiters would be removed by March 1, 1963. This was a very delicate issue because he had to get the other members of NATO to agree to this move without alerting the media that he had made a deal with Khrushchev. Through careful diplomacy, the U.S. was able to convince the Turks and other Europeans that they could be better defended with Polaris submarines than with the out-of-date Jupiters. Kennedy didn't quite meet his deadline but came close. The Jupiters began to be removed in March 1963 and were gone by April 1.

The end of the crisis

From President Kennedy's press conference, November 20, 1962:

"I have been informed by Chairman Khrushchev that all of the IL–28 bombers now in Cuba will be withdrawn in 30 days. He also agrees that these planes can be observed and counted as they leave. Inasmuch as this goes a long way toward reducing the danger which faced this hemisphere four weeks ago, I have this afternoon instructed the Secretary of Defense to lift our naval quarantine."

The Danger of Doomsday

The Cuban Missile Crisis ended peacefully, but it is easy to imagine how things might have gone differently. One of the clearest lessons of the event is the incomplete control Kennedy and Khrushchev held over their militaries. At any moment, a Soviet or U.S. general could have plunged the world into war.

A particularly dangerous moment occurred on October 27, 1962. A U.S. spy plane illegally and accidentally flew into Soviet territory. What was worse, however, was the fact that the U.S. fighter planes sent to steer the pilot back to international airspace, and to protect him from Soviet attack, were armed with nuclear weapons. If an air fight had broken out, or if Khrushchev had learned that nuclear bombers were flying over Soviet territory, it could easily have led to war. In this case, it was clear that Kennedy did not have full control of the U.S. military. The same was true on the Soviet side. War nearly broke out over the U–2 pilot shot down without Khrushchev's approval. And Soviet commanders who controlled nuclear missiles in Cuba were prepared to fire their weapons if the U.S. invaded and communications with Moscow were cut off.

President Kennedy in a thoughtful moment. The world could have easily slipped into war during the Crisis.

On both sides, then, the relationship between the military officials and the civilian politicians was tense. Khrushchev in fact was worried that U.S. military leaders would overthrow Kennedy because of his unwillingness to invade Cuba. Fidel Castro was another source of instability. He was willing to engage in nuclear war in case of a U.S. invasion, and he urged Khrushchev to launch the missiles rather than remove them.

Alternate plans

In another sense, though, the situation was less dangerous than it appeared. Although the U.S. drew up plans for an invasion in case Khrushchev rejected its Saturday night offer, it drew up another, highly secret plan to resolve the crisis peacefully. U Thant, the UN Secretary-General, would have proposed a swap of missiles in Cuba and Turkey if the Soviets had turned down Kennedy's suggestion. This would have been less of a victory for the United States, but at least they would have agreed to a UN resolution rather than followed a Soviet demand. So, despite the real possibility of accidental war, neither Kennedy nor Khrushchev was willing to let violence break out if at all possible to stop it.

The fall of Kennedy and Khrushchev

On November 22, 1963, just a year after the Cuban Missiles Crisis ended, John F. Kennedy was visiting Dallas. As he rode through the city in a convertible, he was shot in the head from a nearby building. Kennedy died and Vice-President Lyndon B. Johnson became president.

A year later, Khrushchev himself fell from power. The Soviet leadership was embarrassed by many of Khrushchev's foreign policy actions, including the Cuban Missile Crisis, and he was replaced by Leonid Brezhnev. Brezhnev was best known for the Brezhnev Doctrine, which declared that the Soviet Union would defend with force any communist country threatened by its neighbors. In this way, the brief period in which John F. Kennedy and Nikita Khrushchev held the fate of the world in their hands came to an end.

The Japanese city of Hiroshima after the U.S. struck it with a nuclear bomb in World War II. The Cuban Missile Crisis came close to repeating this scene in Soviet and U.S. cities.

Russian connection to JFK's death

The man who shot Kennedy was named Lee Harvey Oswald. Although he had lived in the Soviet Union and married a Russian woman, there is no evidence that he was encouraged to kill the president by communists or anyone else. Since Kennedy's assassination, security around U.S. presidents is much tighter when they appear in public.

Changing Historical Views

As with all historical events, views of the Cuban Missile Crisis have varied over the years, especially about the leaders on each side. Kennedy and Khrushchev have each been described either as heroes or villains, depending on the author and on the time in which he or she was writing.

The sixties

After Kennedy was assassinated in 1963, the country went into mourning. He was widely recognized as a great leader killed before his time. Most accounts of the Cuban Missile Crisis published during the remainder of that decade came from former members of Kennedy's own administration or from journalists who knew and worked with him. They drew Kennedy as a heroic figure whose calm and resolution saved the world from nuclear catastrophe. He was seen as a model of how to fight the Cold War and stop the spread of communism, while avoiding the use of military force. Examples of this perspective include Robert Kennedy's book, *Thirteen Days*, published in 1969, and Arthur Schlesinger's *A Thousand Days*. Schlesinger was an advisor to Kennedy, as well as a famous historian whose positive view of the president was very influential.

United States helicopters in Vietnam during the Vietnam war. 58,000 Americans and one million Vietnamese were killed during the Vietnam War.

The revisionists

During the 1970s opinions began to change. The United States fought a very destructive and painful war in Vietnam that challenged many people's attitude toward the Cold War. The idea of containment, which had worked in Europe, was less useful in Southeast Asia. The Kennedy administration was often blamed for beginning U.S. involvement in that war by introducing military "advisors" into Vietnam in 1963. Kennedy's successor, Lyndon B. Johnson, felt he had to continue the commitment of the United States in Southeast Asia because he did not want to abandon a program Kennedy had started.

After Vietnam, a new group of historians and journalists known as "revisionists" were highly critical of Kennedy and his administration. In their view, Kennedy and his advisors were overly aggressive and militaristic. The Cuban Missile Crisis seemed like an unnecessary adventure that brought the world dangerously close to nuclear war for no good reason. Since it was hard to see any difference between the U.S. missiles in Turkey and the Soviet missiles in Cuba, revisionists concluded that Kennedy behaved in a very irresponsible manner. He should have agreed to swap missiles right away, rather than prolong the conflict and risk disaster. By contrast, Khrushchev was portrayed as a noble statesman, willing to back down and save the world, even at the cost of his own political career.

Kennedy signing the Nuclear Test Ban Treaty, an agreement reached in response to the Cuban Missile Crisis.

Contemporary views

More recently, both of these extreme views have been challenged. The national mood in the 70s and 80s was very different from the 50s and 60s. Americans were terrified of communism when Eisenhower and Kennedy were president. Many people believed it was worth risking nuclear war to stop it from spreading. Any politician who could not or would not stand up to communism was seen as weak and ineffective. He would quickly be attacked by members of Congress, newspaper editors, and the general public. Kennedy had no choice but to take a hard line against communism during the 1960 election campaign and during his presidency.

It is now widely believed that Kennedy did a good job handling the Cuban Missile Crisis. Although many people within the administration, the military, the press, and Congress called for an invasion of Cuba no matter what the consequences, Kennedy was able to negotiate a peaceful solution. At the same time, it is clear that Kennedy did not have complete control of the situation. At times military leaders made decisions that could have escalated the crisis or even begun a war, and Kennedy could do nothing about it. The decision to send nuclear bombers to defend a spy plane that wandered into Soviet territory is a good example of that.

The same is true of Khrushchev. Although he bears a good deal of responsibility for beginning the crisis, he was willing to step back from disaster and avoid nuclear war. But the fact that the world was brought so close to nuclear war has hopefully taught us to avoid situations in which nations or military leaders might use nuclear weapons. While Kennedy and Khrushchev were able to avoid war, it is easy to see how they could have failed.

Relations Afterward

The Cold War continued for another 30 years after the Cuban Missile Crisis, but it never again came so close to disaster. In fact, relations between the U.S. and USSR gradually improved. In 1963, Kennedy and Khrushchev signed a nuclear test ban, ending the giant atomic blasts they had recently resumed. During the 1970s, both sides adopted a policy of détente, which meant a relaxing of tensions. The U.S. president, Richard Nixon, and the new Soviet Chairman, Leonid Brezhnev, held SALT I (Strategic Arms Limitation Talks) that pledged to limit the number of nuclear weapons possessed by each side.

Mikhail Gorbachev was the Soviet leader from 1984 to 1991. Most say he ended the Cold War.

The new spirit of cooperation was partly a result of the disaster of the Vietnam War, in which the U.S. attempted to stop the spread of communism in Southeast Asia. After nearly 60,000 Americans and more than one million Vietnamese soldiers and civilians were killed, the U.S. finally pulled out its forces. The communist government of North Vietnam then took control of the entire country.

Enter Gorbachev

During the late 1970s and 1980s, the Cold War warmed up again when President Ronald Reagan increased arms production and the Soviets invaded Afghanistan. Both of these developments placed great strains on the Soviet economy, which had not grown since the late 1960s. In 1982, Brezhnev died and his two successors, Yuri Andropov and Konstantin Chernenko, each held office only for a brief period. In 1985 Mikhail Gorbachev was named chairman. Gorbachev was aware that the Soviet economy was failing and that reforms were necessary. He adopted a policy known as "perestroika" to loosen government control of the economy and make greater use of markets, like in capitalist countries. Gorbachev also promoted "glasnost" or openness. He cut back on censorship of books, films, and newspapers, and released political opponents from prison. He began to make the Communist Party more democratic. In the spring of 1989 free elections were held. At the same time, Gorbachev signed treaties with United States presidents that reduced the number of nuclear weapons held by each side.

The Gorbachev reforms inspired a series of revolutions in Eastern Europe in 1989. In East Germany, the Berlin Wall was torn down, and communist governments in Poland, Czechoslovakia, Hungary, Romania, and Yugoslavia collapsed. In 1991, the Soviet Union itself fell apart. By the mid-1990s, only a handful of communist regimes remained, including North Korea and Cuba.

A lesson learned

The Cold War therefore ended without sparking World War Three. On the other hand, it should not be forgotten that millions of people died in Vietnam, Afghanistan, and elsewhere in Asia, Africa, and South America. They died in wars between communists that were supported by the Soviet Union and anti-communists supported by the United States. By providing weapons, money, and training to non-Europeans, the two sides fought proxy wars to try to spread their systems across the world.

The Cuban Missile Crisis showed how fragile the world is in the nuclear age. A few mistakes could have led to a nuclear disaster. It suggests the importance of having capable people in positions of power on both sides, and it warns of the need to preserve international peace whenever possible.

Germans dance on top of the Berlin Wall in November, 1989. Within a few months, the wall would be torn down and East and West Germany would be reunited.

Timeline

1959	January 1: Fidel Castro takes power in Cuba
1961	January 20: John F. Kennedy becomes the 35th president of the United States
	April 17: Bay of Pigs invasion
	June 3-4: Summit meeting in Vienna between Kennedy and Khrushchev
	August 12: Berlin Wall constructed
	October 30: Soviet Union resumes nuclear tests with the biggest explosion in history
	November: CIA launches "Operation Mongoose"
1962	May 24: The Soviet Union decides to send nuclear missiles to Cuba
	Mid-July: Ships carrying missiles begin to be sent to Cuba
	October 15: Missiles in Cuba are discovered by the CIA
	October 16: Kennedy creates Ex-Comm to discuss how to handle the crisis
	October 22: In a speech to the nation, Kennedy announces U.S. plans to use a naval blockade to force the Soviet Union to remove the missiles
	October 23: The Organization of American States (OAS) approves the U.S. blockade
	October 24: Soviet ships loaded with nuclear weapons turn back to avoid the blockade
	October 25: Stevenson's speech to the United Nations leads to international approval of the blockade
	October 26: The U.S. enforces the blockade for the first time, boarding the *Marcula* at 7:50 a.m.
	October 26: At 6 p.m. the U.S. state department receives Khrushchev's letter hinting at a possible solution to the crisis if the U.S. promises not to invade Cuba
	October 27, morning: Khrushchev sends a second message demanding that the U.S. remove its missiles from Turkey
	October 27: U-2 plane shot down over Cuba. Another U.S. spy plane strays into Soviet airspace. U.S. bombers loaded with nuclear weapons are sent to retrieve the spy plane.
	October 27: Robert Kennedy gives President Kennedy's note accepting Khrushchev's first proposal to Anatoly Dobrynin
	October 28: Khrushchev publicly accepts Kennedy's offer and begins to remove the weapons from Cuba
	November 20: Kennedy lifts the blockade
1963	March 1: The U.S. begins removing Jupiter missiles from Turkey

Further Reading

Brubaker, Paul E. *The Cuban Missile Crisis in American History.* Berkeley Heights, N.J.: Enslow Publishers, 2001.

Chrisp, Peter. *The Cuban Missile Crisis.* Milwaukee, Wisc.: Gareth Stevens, 2002.

Eubank, Keith. *The Missile Crisis in Cuba.* Malabar, FL: Krieger, 2000.

Finkelstein, Norman H. *Thirteen Days/Ninety Miles: The Cuban Missile Crisis.* New York: Julian Messner, 1994.

Medina, Loreta M. (editor). *The Cuban Missile Crisis.* Farmington Hills, Mich.: The Gale Group, 2002.

Ross, Stewart. *The Cuban Missile Crisis: To the Brink of World War III.* Chicago, Ill.: Heinemann Library, 2001.

Sheehan, Sean. *The Cold War.* North Mankato, Minn.: Smart Apple Media, 2003.

Taylor, David. *The Cold War.* Chicago: Heinemann Library, 2001.

Weisbrot, Robert. *Maximum Danger: Kennedy, the Missiles and the Crisis of American Confidence.* Chicago: Ivan R. Dee, 2001.

Glossary

administration United States president and the advisors and officials who help make decisions and run the major departments of the government (Justice, State, Defense, Treasury, Education, Transportation, etc.)

ally a person or nation associated with another in a common purpose

appeasement let someone have his or her way in hopes they will be satisfied

assassination murder of a famous person, usually a political leader

Bay of Pigs place in Cuba where anti-Castro rebels landed in 1961. They were defeated and captured when the United States did not help them.

blockade close off a place to prevent coming in or going out of people or supplies

Bolshevik Party Communist Party of Russia that came to power in 1917 under the leadership of Vladimir Lenin

bureaucracy the many people and departments of a company or institution, usually in government. Individual people are called *bureaucrats.*

capitalism system in which land ownership and wealth is owned mostly by private individuals

Central Intelligence Agency (CIA) organization of United States spies who gather information about foreign governments

Cold War 40-year struggle for influence and power between the United States and its capitalist and democratic allies, and the Soviet Union and its communist allies

colony a group of people sent by a country to settle in a new territory

communism government of the working-class that aims at equality for all individuals, and in which means of production are held by the government

concession something granted or given

Dardanelles narrow waterway in Turkey between the Mediterranean Sea and the Black Sea. Important for Soviet shipping.

defect give up one's country for another because of a change in thinking

depth charge underwater explosives directed at submarines

deputy person appointed to act for or in place of another

détente relaxing of tensions between the United States and the Soviet Union, beginning in the late 1960s and continuing into the 1970s

dictatorship government in which one person rules with total authority

diplomat government worker whose job is to keep good relations with other countries

Executive Committee of the United States Security Council (Ex Comm) group of Kennedy's closest foreign affairs advisors asked to find a solution to the Cuban Missile Crisis

exile person who is expelled from his or her country, usually for political reasons

KGB (Committee for State Security) Soviet version of the CIA

Gulag Archipelago system of prisons and labor camps where opponents of the Soviet government were sent and which were meant to speed industrialization of the Soviet Union

hypocritical having two standards for one matter; saying one thing and doing another

Jupiters missiles placed in Italy and Turkey during the 1950s and early 1960s to defend Europe from a Soviet attack. They were removed from Turkey in 1963 after the Soviets pulled their missiles out of Cuba.

missile gap belief many Americans held in the late 1950s that the Soviet Union had more nuclear weapons than the United States

Monroe Doctrine claim that no European powers should interfere in the affairs of countries located in the western hemisphere

Munich Conference and Agreement 1938 arrangement that allowed Hitler to take over part of Czechoslovakia in order to avoid war. This policy was known as "appeasement."

naval blockade surrounding an area with ships to prevent people or goods from getting in. During the Cuban Missile Crisis the United States preferred to use the term "quarantine."

negotiate discuss with another in order to settle something

nuclear of or being a weapon whose destructive power comes from splitting of the atom

nuclear test experiment with nuclear weapons often held on small deserted islands

Operation Mongoose CIA's attempt to overthrow Castro's government by encouraging sabotage, rebellion, or assassination

Organization of American States (OAS) group of nations in North and South America that tries to manage events in the western hemisphere

Polaris submarine submarine that can fire nuclear weapons

policy course of action chosen to guide people in making decisions

proxy wars use of another country or army to fight a war

purge to get rid of. In politics, it usually means to eliminate rivals.

quarantine halt or forbid moving of people or things out of or into a certain area

rebel being or fighting against one's government or ruler

regime government

revisionist person who looks something over again to correct or improve it

Russian Revolution 1917 revolution when the Czar, the royal ruler, was overthrown, and the Bolsheviks under Lenin took power and set up communism

Soviet Union (USSR) communist country from 1917 to 1991 that was made up of Russia and several neighboring territories

sword of Damocles refers to a story in Greek mythology in which a sword held up by a single hair hangs over a man's head, and the slightest movement could kill him. The phrase refers to any very dangerous or threatening situation.

totalitarianism political system in which the individual is secondary to the government, which strictly controls all aspects of life

Truman Doctrine United States policy started in the Truman administration to defend any U.S. allies threatened by a communist government or movement

United Nations (UN) organization created after World War II to encourage peace and fight poverty, hunger, and disease

U-2 large spy plane equipped with cameras that the United States uses to collect information on other countries

warhead the part of a missile carrying the explosive charge

World War II war between Germany, Japan, and Italy vs. Britain, France, the Soviet Union, and the United States (and many other countries, too) that lasted from 1939 to 1945

Vietnam country in Southeast Asia where the United States fought a long but unsuccessful war from 1965 to 1973 to prevent the spread of communism

vindicate to free from blame or guilt, or show to be true and correct

Index